Foul Ball!

by Joaquin Garcia
illustrated by Lyle Miller

Core Decodable 99

I0806534

McGraw Hill Education

Bothell, WA • Chicago, IL • Columbus, OH • New York, NY

MHEonline.com

Send all inquiries to:
McGraw-Hill Education
8787 Orion Place
Columbus, OH 43240

ISBN: 978-0-02-145299-6
MHID: 0-02-145299-7

Printed in the United States of America.

7 8 9 LCR 25 24 23

Paul looked down in awe at the baseball field. It was so green. "Wow!" said Paul to Gramps.

Lots of fans sat around Paul. The fans all came to see the Owls play the Hawks.

The Owls were the town's team. The Owls played at Brown Park.

Paul was thrilled because it was hard to get Owls tickets. But Gramps had found a way.

"I like these seats," said Paul. "We could catch a foul ball."

"Maybe," said Gramps.

Gramps had seen lots of Owls games. But Gramps never got a foul ball.

Soon the game started. The crowd applauded. Fans squawked, "Go, Owls, go!"

The best hitter was up. The pitch was fast. Pow! He launched the ball way up!

It was a high foul ball. The ball flew in the stands close to Paul and Gramps!

But the ball did not reach them. Paul saw it hit a cement step. It made a loud sound as it bounced.

The foul ball bounced by Paul. Now was his chance.

Paul got the foul ball! Gramps felt proud.

"How about that catch!" shouted Gramps.

Paul looked at the ball. Paul looked at Gramps.

Paul held the round ball for a second. Then he gave it to Gramps.

"This ball is for you, Gramps," said Paul.

Gramps smiled and gave it back.
"No thanks, Paul," said Gramps.
Gramps felt even prouder of Paul.